# Hoggo's Online Adventure

## A Hedgehog's Journey in Cybertown!

Written by

**Noa Kahalon**

Designed and Illustrated by

**Valery Uryvska (Valetery)**

Hoggo the Hedgehog loves adventures. One day, he wanders into Cybertown, an online world accessible through our laptops, tablets, and phones. During his journey to Cybertown, Hoggo learns about the dangers lurking in the online world, such as cyberbullying, impersonators, phishing, and dangers to privacy.

Join Hoggo as he overcomes the challenges and dangers of the online world.

The goal of this book is to teach children how to use the internet and apps safely, while also having fun!

Text written by Noa Kahalon
Designed and illustrated by Valery Uryvska

ISBN 978-1-3999-8172-9

Copyright © 2024 by Noa Kahalon
All rights reserved

Hoggo was a hedgehog...
A hedgehog who loved to roam.
He yearned to visit strange new worlds
and wanders far from home.

He'd been to Africa and Spain,
Greece, Belgium, and Dubai.
He'd seen the Eiffel Tower,
The Great Wall and London Eye.

He'd even had adventures
in places you'd think were fake:
Cake Mountain and The Underworld,
Cloud Land, and The Magic Lake.

And at the time our story starts,
Hoggo was off again
to explore the online world,
where there is no need for a plane.

The online world is in laptops,
tablets and phones. But is it?
Well, yes, but also, it's a place
that small hedgehogs can visit.

See, Hoggo was just small enough
to fit without a squeeze.
He'd slip right through
the USB port with
surprising ease.

But before setting off for online pastures new and nice,
His parents stopped him and served up some piping hot advice.

"I know," said Momma Hog,
"that you have been to places before.
But the online world has dangers you should not ignore."

"I know," said Poppa Hog,
"that some things will look flash, fun, and bright.
But they still may pose danger, kid.
They might not be quite right."

"So, use your spikes.
Protect yourself.
Be wary of the threat.
Of all your journeys, this may be the most perilous yet!"

Despite his parents' warnings,
Hoggo wasn't scared at all.
"Nothing!" Hoggo said,
"will have me roll into a ball!"

Excited Hoggo wriggled through
the small USB port.
"This will be the best adventure yet!"
young Hoggo thought.

He popped through...
'POP!'
...just like a cork
      and bumped into a sign.
        "Welcome to Cybertown!" it read.
          "A world that's all online!"

After roaming around a while,
taking each sound and site,
Hoggo was hungry and looked for a place to
have a byte.

'The Social Media Café' had
five stars in the Town Guide.
But the great big guard spider
stopped strangers sneaking inside.

"Can I come in?" asked Hoggo.
"I've an appetite and thirst!"
"You can," sneered Spider.
"But you must give me a few things first."

"Not much, of course; only your name,
number and where you live.
Some dreams and fears unique to you.
That's all you need to give!"

"That seems a lot for just one visit,"
Hoggo told the spider.
"Your details are like cash," said Spider.
"In the world of cyber."

"We use it to show you the things
that we want you to see.
And ads for things that make you
send real cash from you to me!"

"NO THANKS!" yelped Hoggo, leaping back.
"Entry's not worth the trade.
Especially with all the nastiness
you have just displayed!"

Still starving, Hoggo kept an eye out
for some tasty dish.
And soon he passed a fisherman,
who offered him some fish.

"Come over here, my spiky friend.
Take this fish from my fist.
It's fresh and fried and piping hot.
Surely, you can't resist."

The fisherman seemed charming.
And the food looked quite the catch.
But when Hoggo got close,
away from him the meal was snatched!

"You stupid hedgehog!"
said the fisherman, grabbing his arm.
"They call me Phishy.
Best beware, for I may cause you harm!"

"Now... give me all your usernames
and passwords!" Phishy screamed.
"You sneaky sailor!" Hoggo yelled.
"You're not the friend you seemed!"

"I'll have them all," sneered Phishy.
"And break into your accounts.
Inject malware and nasty bugs
in enormous amounts!"

Hoggo used his spikiest bits
to prod him in the face.
So, Phishy bellowed and let go.
Hoggo ran from that place!

"I saw that," a kind badger said.
"That Phishy is a brute!
Always trying to trick folk
by seeming kind or cute."

"Don't worry, friend.
You come with me.
I'm off to join a party.
I'll show you Cybertown's a joy!
I'll feed you something hearty."

At last, our Hoggo had found someone
he could truly trust.
In Cybertown, that's hard to find.
But safety is a must.

The party was fantastic.
There were foods of crazy kinds...
like 'Mega Bites' and 'Nano Nuts',
'Roast RAMs' and 'Wi-Fi Wines'.

The music, it was poppin'.
So, Hoggo began to bop.
But he bumped into a bull,
whose temper blew up with a 'POP!'

"LOOK WHERE YOU'RE GOING, PINHEAD!"
yelled the bull, bursting with rage.
"NOBODY DANCE OR PLAY WITH HIM!"
he yelled out from the stage.

And though it was an accident,
the bull had meant it fully.
He turned the party against him.
The bull was... well, a bully.

But Hoggo would not let it get to him.
He shouted out,
'That bull's a bully.
A disgrace!
Of that, there's no doubt!"

With sadness, he then left the party.
Hoggo knew not to stay.
He knew that when things got sour,
the best thing was to walk away.

So far, Hoggo was feeling sad
about his trip online.
But now he knew what not to do.
He knew things would be fine.

And so, from then, with every choice,
to himself, he would say...
"My momma told me, when in doubt,
there's no doubt. Walk away!"

After his rocky start online,
Hoggo enjoyed the place.
He safely watched cat videos.
Put filters on his face.

He found pictures,
discovered songs,
and messaged his hog friends.
He played fun games where he scored points
and unearthed hidden gems.

When Hoggo came back from his trip,
he knew what he should do...
He wrote a list of rules and tips
for me to share with you.

The online world is super fun,
but as you all have seen,
to have the fun, we must be safe,
when doing stuff on screen.

Turn this page over, and you will find
the rules that Hoggo wrote.
They're there for you to use online.
Make sure that you take note.

**Number One!**
Don't give out data
that's private to you.
You don't know what they'll use it for.
You don't know what they'll do!

**Number Two!**
Some people who
pretend to be good guys
aren't nice at all! So, walk away
if there's a whiff of lies!

**Number Three!**
Get your spikes up
if online bullies come!
And point the finger.
Call them out!
Tell others they are scum!

**Number Four!**
Don't meet people
from the online world on your own.
They could be anybody.
Do not be with them alone.

**Last, Number Five!**
Have a great time!
Adventure has begun!
So, pop your spikes up and enjoy.
The internet is fun!

## Written by Noa Kahalon

Noa Kahalon is an entrepreneur,
privacy advocate, and author dedicated
to making the online world a safer place.
Her background is a distinct blend of law, marketing,
business, and technology.
As a co-founder of hoggo.io, a privacy-tech startup,
Noa actively works towards fostering transparency in
businesses' data privacy practices.
vvMotivated by her experiences,
Noa wrote this book to raise awareness about the
hidden dangers of the digital landscape and to teach
children how to navigate it safely. In this age of
unprecedented digital connectivity, her focus remains on
empowering both adults and children to explore
the online world responsibly.

hoggo

www.ingramcontent.com/pod-product-compliance
Lightning Source LLC
Chambersburg PA
CBRC090838010526
44118CB00007B/245